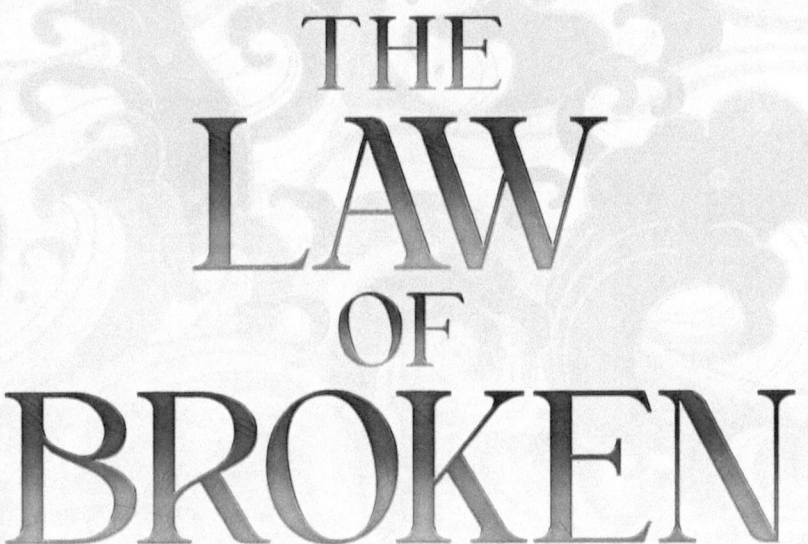

THE LAW OF BROKEN

APRIL SAVAGE

Copyright © 2026 April Savage

All rights reserved.

No portion of this book may be reproduced in any form without written permission from the publisher or author, except as permitted by U.S. copyright law.

Cover designed by Getcovers

Contents

The Power of Poetry	VII
Where We Hope	1
1. The Silence of Screams	2
2. This is Not How it Should Be	4
3. It Matters	7
4. Breathing Freeness	10
5. The Day the World Broke	13
6. The Day the World Healed	14
7. The Anguish of Falling	16
8. Bleeding Sight	17
9. Even Over There	18
10. Sometimes Pain	20
11. The Freeing	22
12. The Chance	24
13. Just Go Live	25

The World is Screaming	27
14. Small	28
15. The Sun	30
16. Gentle Rain	32
17. Mother Nature	34
18. Wind	36
19. The Pond	38
20. Imagination of Storms	40
21. The Old Barn	41
22. Dying Ember	43
23. Summer Storm	44
24. Look Harder	46
25. The Soul of Me	49
26. The Secret Within	51
27. The Small Things	53
28. Bigger than Me	55
When the Heart Aches	57
29. When the Bed Gets Cold	58
30. Breathe the Flower	61
31. Loved Like a Stone	64

32.	I Kept my Spine	66
33.	No I Don't	68
34.	The Obsession	70
35.	The Lie of Time	73
36.	The Moaning of Hope	75
37.	Dreams	76
38.	The Heartbreak	77
39.	Unfulfilled Thoughts	78
40.	The Last Time	79
41.	The Capture	81
	The Awakening	82
42.	Expressions of Silence	83
43.	Terrified	84
44.	A Neighboring Hope	86
45.	My History Ashamed	90
46.	Rekindled	92
47.	The Persuasion	95
48.	Prism of Darkness	97
49.	Feed the Machine	99
50.	The Soul of Writing	101

51.	How Can I Serve You?	103
52.	Maps of Lies	107
53.	Tired Empire	109
54.	How Not to See	114
55.	Dust of my Bones	117
56.	Burn it Off	123
57.	Spark the Flame	126
58.	The Law of Broken	127

The Power of Poetry

Words carry meaning and hope

Words can also cut and hurt like stone

The power of words can build humanity

Or tear it down

The power of words can encourage and empower

Poetry breathes life in shorter stories,

but with precision and power

Poetry summons seeds to grow deep inside,

and enhance our minds

The power of poetry will never die

so here I am,

spilling my soul in everything I write

PART I: WHERE WE HOPE

The Silence of Screams

There's a wall there

I stand facing it

My hope claims the other side

My heart aches,

but I get over the wall

and the hill is steep and lonely

I see the horizon

and it rolls and flows like a river,

so, I go there

My legs ache and burn,

my back is worn down

but I stand to face the mountain

It looms to the sky

and shadows over my intentions

It writhes and storms,

stomping on my ambitions

I wail and scream

and pull my hopes from my dreams

to climb the mountain

As I reach the peak,

the clouds kiss my aches and pains

My hopes and dreams I reclaim,

because although I wailed and screamed

and writhed in pain,

my silent ambitions remained

This is Not How it Should Be

It shouldn't be this way

hunger, pain, and malicious drought,

and then endless rain to wash it all out

It shouldn't be greedy or hopeless

It shouldn't be wicked

with lack of remorsefulness

It shouldn't be stifled or imprisoned unjustly

and held back with no way out

There should not be a lack of justice

or reprieve

A lack of un-thoughtfulness unseen

There should never be a hopeless abandon

or unending sorrows of no reprieve

But,

this is what should be...

There should be singing and dancing

and triumphant overcoming of once dead dreams

There should be hope for tomorrow

provision and rest

There should always be justice

and thoughtful help for the weary to heal

and if that isn't well enough,

well then, life's just hell

But is it enough?

Because we can give all this and more

Humanity should not operate

like we are in the pits of the darkest night

or the depths of unending maliciousness

We can feed the hungry

and provide for the helpless

We can breathe a flaming hope

for those who are weary and weak,

because this is not how it should be

It Matters

If I died today

would any of this would matter, you think

writhing on the brink,

you carry great pain and despair you can no longer bear

you contemplate your path

and want to kill your dreams, thinking you have none at all

But it matters

because a moment of time can make a difference

It matters

because our choices can cause peace or division

Every little thing we do

has consequence

Every little thing we do

isn't just about me or you

Actions can bring about peace

or war

Actions can stir a season of drought

or a flood of unending sorrow

It can breathe life back into doom

and the hopeless tomorrow

and what we once thought was gone forever

can give the living a clinging reprieve

When everything seems to be lost

Read

this

out

loud

and put your choice of weapon down

Whatever you are doing that will bring great harm

Stop what you are doing right now,

and breathe the truth of hope

Because you matter

You have always mattered

If you leave now

a light will blow out

It will not be rekindled

It will not cast a shadow

upon a lonely wall or upon anything at all

The light of you will be gone forever

And although the world will carry on,

the purpose of your soul will leave a scar

There is no hopeless tomorrow
as long as you are breathing
You are here for a reason,
doesn't matter if it's just a season

Breathing Freeness

I breathed once

when I was free,

but an obsidian shroud

empowered the night

already consuming my world

and it took me

and drove me to my knees

It took me

to mold me and put me in chains

It took me to keep me

So, I stopped breathing

and died inside

I stopped breathing

and my hope subsided

Darkness is not only seen

it is felt

Darkness moves with delight

and consumes dreams

But something else grew

in the pit of my night

Something else grew

to pull me from my plight

It was not seen

but it breathed

It did not scream, but it schemed

It was more treacherous

than the darkest of nights

It grew spines of malice

and thorns of division

It sprouted wings of decision

with its empowering vision

It ripped the darkness wide open

and brought back my hope

It pulled me from the oppression

giving me a sword

to cut the shroud that stole my breath

So, I breathe again

and stand here, ready to fight

I breathe again, and live here,

to help deliver others from this plight

I will continue living to fight the night

The Day the World Broke

It spent its time struggling to survive

In the smallest flower that breathes the dew

In the tangly vines that consume anew

Everything that lives and breathes

in our world is pure majesty

The day the world broke

is when compassion fled and burned high hopes

The day it broke

is when hate filled vengeance

screamed for blood and consumed everything

I guess the world has always been broke

But it doesn't have to be

The Day the World Healed

It started with a hopeful wonder

of stubborn perseverance

It began in the hearts of those

who were tired of grief

So, they gathered together

and built a powerful reprieve

They stood together

and formed a bridge of splendor

They fought for the right to breathe

and heal others who were suffocating

The day the world healed

is when mankind

began walking together

and building a world

for the weak and those who could not fight

So, the world can heal

if we choose to work together

to make it better

The Anguish of Falling

It's okay to trip and fall

Obstacles can make us bleed

and make us see

When the darkness comes,

its pressure weighs upon us like crushing bones

To feel anything is being alive

Even though darkness is so heavy,

the pressure from its oppression

builds and eventually blows

And that's when the light finds you

Bleeding Sight

Just because you cannot see it

doesn't mean it cannot thrive

Just because you cannot feel it

doesn't mean it is not alive

Sometimes our eyes only go so far

Sometimes our hearts refuse

to go any further at all

And just because there is a wall there

doesn't mean it cannot be torn down

It doesn't mean that is the end of your journey

or that there is nothing beyond it

There is something beyond everything

There is always a way

Even Over There

They didn't say there would be so much sorrow

But they knew it everywhere,

even over there

They did say our own kind would be cruel and malicious

And we are, even over there

Over there lies a writhing darkness

billowing like a stormy hell

Raging pain creeps in, screaming through the rain

everywhere

But they did tell me the heart is veracious,

brave and strong

They did tell me hope billows stronger

than any raging storm

THE LAW OF BROKEN

They warned me when the time comes

to stand up for what is right

that the heart rages like a lion,

it roars, and fights

It doesn't give up

Even over there

Sometimes Pain

Sometimes pain cannot be described

It is heavy like dread

and takes time to heal

It's okay to cry and even kneel

Sometimes pain is the worst of us all

because it digs in, doesn't give up at all

Sometimes pain isn't physical

It's a nameless whisper that's gaudy and tall

It's a shadowless claim of unending horror

It breaks you wide open and hollows out your heart

then it comes back for more whether you want it to or not

Sometimes pain is a moment of time that lingers on

and there's nothing you can do about it until you are gone

But sometimes pain

sprouts a seed within us like a gentle wind

and grows in silence until it wins

Sometimes pain teaches us to be strong and stand tall

even when we had nothing to help us at all

The Freeing

Write and get it out

Paint and spill your pains

Run and shake your fears

Build and breathe stone

Walk and burn it off

Cry and let it in

Moan and break

Grieve and forsake

Fall and scrape

It's okay to feel like giving up

It's not okay

for anyone to devalue your worth

or smash your hopes

It's not okay for anyone to stifle your talents

and dash your dreams

It's okay to just be you

The Chance

Lay the chance

give it time

Then bless it

with nourishment,

so, it can grow and flourish

in the hands of time

Just Go Live

You may watch the sun come up

over rolling hills, mountains or plateaus

You may work in the city

Every person is different in their own way

every person has perspectives

that may never change

Life can be simple or busy

and full of purpose and plenty

Whether you live in the country

or a bustling, busy city

Go live your life

because we are not promised tomorrow

Whether it is the silence of country living

or the sprawling buildings

Whether you crave sunrises over hills

or the skyline of a city

Just go live

that is the point of it all

PART II:
THE WORLD IS SCREAMING

Small

The world is big and beautiful

the universe is vast and intricate

but you wouldn't know it

because humans continue to judge one another

for their curves or slenderness

for their big or small breasts

for the color of their skin

or what they do best

and even what lies within

Humans plot and conceive

the vilest things

and then point the finger

when their judgement continues to berate

Whether you have curves or are slender

whether you have the ideal perfect figure

it doesn't matter

because this world is a big place

and although judgement steals and takes

you were made to be who you are

no matter what

the universe is a grand place, after all

and humans are very, very small

The Sun

You,

bursting through the clouds,

pouring all over the emerald fields.

With the rain shattering your life,

you always break through,

pushing your enemies away.

The evil world

of puffy clouds shadow under you,

ruining your will to stay air born.

Over the sea,

you spread your diamonds,

glistening in the world under the watery grave.

The birds fly with you, and soar free,

under your calm masterpiece.

Gentle Rain

The gentle rain makes me feel like a dew drop clinging to a wet leaf

It fills the bright flowers bed and soaks it all in,

providing life to all that inhabit the landscape

Gentle rain falls so gently upon the earth,

and gives me a feeling of tranquility

Gentle rain pours delicately over the beautiful green fields

The puffy clouds push their way open,

forcing tiny buckets of drops out of the mighty heavens

The droplets spill out, and one by one,

my hair becomes soaked

Gentle rain lets me sleep and I dream gentle fantasies

Gentle rain is beautiful to me

and it fills my soul with creativity

Mother Nature

You have the moon on your cheek

The sky is your heavenly blue eyes

The trees are your arms reaching into infinity

The seas are your music,

gently playing within the crowded arms of your life

The sun shares with you your beauty

The creatures within are your guests,

you are the host-

sheltering them from man's evil ways

You invite in only the gentlest of humans,

a soul with pure intentions and no evil intended

The darkness surrounding you at night

is your cape you pull to hide from it

Yet you still keep watch

And sometimes, within the misty night,

I can see your gray eyes watching me

Wind

Wind...

        Softly sailing

gently swaying

    lowly laying

quietly waiting

          certainly hating

    freshly biting

       coldly longing

             boldly exploring

        heavenly withholding

             sharply stabbing

        carefully planning

    lonely having

        homely wanting

              lessly becoming

                        WIND

The Pond

The restless waters

ripple and sway

from shore to shore,

pushing a gray aura onto the grass.

       Old, crinkly cat tails stand tall

        and pour out over the crystal waters.

          Tiny minnows frantically

scamper

in a race to their deaths

as a baby pine tree stands along the edge

leaving a lingering shadow

        in the restless waters.

THE LAW OF BROKEN

    Birds glide within its cool breeze

        and settle down on bushy cat tails.

            In the sun, the pond glistens

                    and sparkles

  ferociously

                as its depth is

            uncovered.

Imagination of Storms

When the rain pours and the trees sway

and shattered strikes of lightening

echo through the great sky,

I see a marvelous sight

I see a warrior with a whip in one hand

beating the trees, and in his other hand,

he grips bolts of lightening

from which he shoots up into the sky,

and out of his mouth spurts the cold, hard rain

which we all run for shelter to escape it

The Old Barn

Silently you linger within the vast forest

surrounding your patient heart.

You will sit and rot until someone comes along

with some love and restores you.

But your family will not restore you,

they would rather build a new barn.

The oak trees next to you are dying slowly too,

and yet, still, you wait.

Like a figment of the imagination,

you pop out to a visitor

as the black sky pokes and prods

around you like an evil abyss tearing

at your feeble strips of eaten wood.

But you are still there.

I wish you'd just fall down,

giving you a reprieve of peace in death.

You will be there even after I am gone,

lingering on and on.

I hate you are dilapidated,

but am forced to watch you rot.

Dying Ember

You cast an eerie orange shadow

across the stone fireplace

as emptiness fills the expansive, bare room.

A dying ember

slowly emerges from the grave,

spewing uncertainty upon the wall.

Snuffed out,

losing your graceful touch of warmth,

delicately you die

and the room becomes a dark masterpiece.

Summer Storm

Gleams from bursts of lightening

pound the dreary sky.

Two Sycamore trees stand tall,

thrashing as cracks of lightening attack them.

The cold, wet air deposits endless drops of rain,

cascading upon the bare fields.

The wind sits still, awaiting the command to howl.

Suddenly, the rain stops, becoming heavier.

Cries of thunder echo throughout the whole universe.

The rain becomes a falling masterpiece,

attacking at a steadier speed.

The colorful array of flowers pours out,

sucking from the falling rain.

The wind carries a song of silence as bold

lightning strikes are seen atop the green summer trees.

Look Harder

If we linger longer in this world

We should look harder at the clouds

and let our eyes explore the heavens

whether there be rainbows or darkness

We should look harder

at how waves form on sand

and how the oceans kiss the land

We should look harder

at the plains and valleys

and the looming mountains

to see how small we really are

We should look harder

at how a spider can weave a web

of intricate beauty cloaked in death

or how the creatures of the woodlands

live their lives until their last breaths

We should look harder

at flowers and the perfection of their peace

or just sit to enjoy silence

or even the joy of children's playful screams

There is no reason to live this short life

if we do not stop and breathe

if we do not stop and feel a need to be at peace

There is no point to existence

if we cannot just be

So, look harder,

tiny human,

look harder with all you can,

because one day

you'll wish you looked harder

until your time comes up

The Soul of Me

It's not a human

not an animal

It's not the sea

or the clouds roaring above me

It's not even the rain

or whatever pain haunts me

It's not a simple thing

that lives inside me

It's a conquest of meticulous splendor

It's a hope of magnificent wonder

It cannot be described

only felt

It cannot be stopped

but it is tender

It cannot be seen

but it lingers

It cannot be heard

but the breath of it screams inside me

It billows and quakes

It grows and shakes

It doesn't give up easily

It conquers and creates

It cannot be described effectively

because it is a breath living inside me

The Secret Within

Within a vast number of crowded trees

lies the waiting of an archeological finding,

something worth turning back for,

something prying eyes dare not miss.

The secret within

displays mysteries of a powerful touch in the

life of nature itself.

It is a wondrous sight to finally reach the climax

of a hard and sweaty journey,

leading to uncover vast treasures within.

This secretive valley engulfs like an empty shield barrier.

With a quick rest, and hard weapons,

mankind strips this once pristine forest from her greenery.

A gorgeous velvety lining thriving

in and out from the heart of this mystical forest,

is now gone, even as treasures are taken.

The Small Things

It's not a small thing

but easy to think it is sometimes

It's not a big deal until we make it one

Sometimes the small things

are like feathers, soft and flowy

but designed with purpose

Sometimes the small things

leave lasting impressions

It's the small things that matter

because life is hard no matter where you strive

It could be a simple flower

or a smile from lingering eyes

It could be a flash summer storm

brewing in dark skies

Maybe it's just the hope of tomorrow

and the endless dreams we keep

Maybe it's just a simple pleasure

of food, comfort, and keep

Perhaps it's just a moment in time

of silence and rest

Sometimes it's the small things

that are big and tall

Every waking moment is a big deal

until it is time to die

or even heal

Because at the end of our lives

it's the small things we linger upon

It's the small things

that draw us on

Bigger than Me

I stand as it comes for me

roaring and shaking

It flows and brakes

Then it pulls back until it takes

It rolls and crashes

screaming as it lashes

Then it is calm as a whisper

and always clever

It sings and dances

as it consumes and hates

It beckons like a seductive charm

It eats like a monster of the deep

And though my heart craves its power

I step back to admire it

This is the sea

and it is bigger than me

It will always be bigger than me

PART III:
WHEN THE HEART ACHES

When the Bed Gets Cold

We spent years holding and loving

caressing and giving

We spent years breathing one another's

hopes upon our lips

We took the time to grow

with one another and not give up

we took the time to overcome hardships

but we did it together

We took the time to build our dreams for one another

and every night we held one another close

and filled up of each other's hopes

and every night we bled dreams til waking dawn

and the sun was ours to keep

Until one day,

you were gone

You were gone and not coming back

You were gone and that was that

The bed got cold

but my love remained

The bed got cold

but my hope continues to reclaim

When I close my eyes

I still see your splendor,

and your heart breathes inside me

When I close my eyes

your breaths are still in my ear

The bed may be cold

but you continue lingering near

so, I lie here

and continue growing old

until one day I join you in our hopeful song

One day,

this whole bed will be cold

and I will lie with you again under the sun,

because you were taken from me too soon

but until then,

I carry on

Breathe the Flower

You won't even pluck it up to kill it

or bend to smell its enticing aroma

You won't even breathe in its beauty or its pain

or take the time to see how it thrives in the rain

You won't even glance its way

to admire the intricateness of its creation

or the thought of its peace

You refuse to sit and linger

because there is no wonder or hope with your fingers

It only takes a moment to stop and breathe

Your mind is chasing matters that will not give you hope

Your heart clings to a future that will not bring you peace

There is only this moment

and I am here now for you

But you are gone again chasing the world

and leaving me to wonder

So, if you cannot even stop to breathe the flowers

then why do I want you for a mate?

Why would I crave your soul to take?

Why would I pursue this catastrophe

that is you, you,

the one who chases everything in the world

besides the flowers I take in,

the one who pursues relentless adventures

that have nothing to do with my heart

You just want my skin and pleasure

You just want what I can give you, even for later

You can't even ask me if I want to come along

You treat me as if I am grounded like the flowers

and cannot be plucked up and planted elsewhere

You won't even pursue

the love I have for you in a song

So, you will reap and sow what you pursue

and the flowers will continue to grow

in their magnificent splendor

And I will, too

Loved Like a Stone

Give me a rose for eternity

Bless me with a smile from the heart

Give me a promise you can't take back

Love me with a love like no other

Bless me with a hug by strong, loving arms

Give me a kiss by eager lips

Love me with a time never meant to be broken

A ring is given to pronounce dedication,

yet even roses die once you pick them

and something that beautiful is also powerful in death

Smiles can be fake or twisted, and even sick

Hugs can be shallow and mean

and kissing is many things

Diamonds may last forever

but even a ring of expectation

cannot outlast the stormy weather

When it comes to the heart,

it's not a game, nor a place to play

The heart is something that sometimes,

refuses to stay

I Kept my Spine

I walked among the folds of lingering meadows

and danced as the sun kissed me

I fed my hopes, and my soul was rested

I never questioned my looks, my desires, or lust

But then you came and set your eyes upon me

You came and enticed me to follow

and I stopped walking among the life I loved so much

I lost myself when you came

because you sought me as if I were a priceless treasure

for you to plunder and take and do whatever

In time, I knew I would rather die lonely than in your grasp

and I learned many priceless treasures aren't truly loved,

nor do they last, they are only kept

THE LAW OF BROKEN

So, you took me like a priceless treasure,

and grew weary with greed

as you sought something bigger with your needs

But I still had my hope and silence giving me a reprieve

I still have me, and now I see that I am enough

One day, you cast me off

and I found myself roaming my old fields again

hiding from ones like you

I stayed hidden for ages until I grew anew

and I emerged again with eagle eyes and wings of fervor

I faced the world with my own magnificent splendor

So, when another came with eyes set upon me

I laughed at the lust and the aching sorrows

I laughed at the purpose of its demise

I turned and walked away

and this time, I kept my spine

No I Don't

I don't have to wear lies

to please you

I don't have to breathe envy

to keep you

I don't have to live false hopes

to persuade you

I don't need to fake a smile

to please you

I don't have to look you in the eyes

to acknowledge you

I don't need to justify myself

or who I am to keep you

I used to care what you thought of me

but now I don't

you don't care for me at all

If you cared for me,

you would wear truth

like a double-edged sword

You would breathe in hope

and appreciate my smile

You would meet my eyes

and look inside,

and there would be no justification

to set our friendship aside

But you won't,

so, no I don't

The Obsession

The time is nigh, the time is now,

you've lived it all but forgotten it somehow

You've dreamed great dreams and remembered the past,

but time is at your door, and it's never meant to last

Through shattered memories and tormented nightmares,

you've cried out and tread on some lonesome stones,

and knowing you, you've been alone through the fires

and in your aching pains, tried to forgive yourself

amongst all the worlds evil, greedy lust

Now that time is up, will you ever go back?

Or ever grow up?

I could give you words to say,

but I can't make your pain go away

THE LAW OF BROKEN

I can hold your hand and caress your lips

and do all the things you've ever dreamed

of in your cerebral abyss

But, through your broken heart, I can't mend,

walking alone, I can't follow your ways

Crying out, I can't hear your shattered emotions

You've got to break the barriers,

bust the dams, and do what is right

and live the time left for you

Throughout all your life, you've lived for you

You've known nothing else

Time is true, I swear it to you

You've sacrificed for unwanted treasures,

because of your addictions

and unhealthy, lustful measures

You can Love now or refuse truth and die alone

But choose, because time is calling,

and your obsessions will die with you

The Lie of Time

Time has freed my mind

and allowed me to travel once again

upon these lonesome stones

of my never-ending quest for life

Time has granted me

peace and blessed me with hopes and dreams

never conquered by my own mind

Time itself has caused

deep hysteria within my broken heart

to be held and caressed by empty feelings of hate

Time has seen

wonders and miracles within my very soul,

miracles bursting forth with a great light

that cries out and then slowly dies

But for a time, if only for a moment,

I could reach out and touch that part of me,

a secret destroyer, now lost,

and mend those torn pages to my novel life,

only then I would free myself

and then time would release the prisoner

and I could be myself once again

The Moaning of Hope

It trickles

and moans

It rages

and burns

to the endless abyss

It breathes and seethes

and kisses

as it dreams

And sometimes

when it seems darkness has overcome

it rips the deep wide open

and roars

Dreams

I reach out for you,

my hands grabbing any part to your empty silhouette

But my fingers glide right through you

I run toward you,

my legs burning from the swiftness of how fast I try

But I reach nothing

And though I race like the speed of light toward you,

I run into an abyss of never-ending dreams,

dreams I cannot touch

dreams I cannot run to

The Heartbreak

I looked into your eyes and turned to sand

all my dreams came true

the moment we said we do

Vows of love and lives of fear

taking chances left so unclear

You never understood the choice you made

Now, I'm left standing here so alone

The vow that winter had turned so cold

frozen and hard, into your world of ice

I'll never be the same

it'll never go away

to believe I was no naive,

and you, so brave

Unfulfilled Thoughts

The gates of time

age against the wind

as nightmares roar

into unfulfilled thoughts

retracing their natural roots

in the lonely folds of the mind

as part of a thought is kept back

for fear of loosening,

sending an unfulfilled thought

into a fulfilling mind

and that's where the story begins

The Last Time

He died the last time I saw him

I cried over him, but he was already gone

My mind replayed moments and memories

My mind replayed our hopes and dreams

and every little moment in between

I cried myself to sleep

I kept the sound of his heartbeat

Now I look around

and see people running from their dreams

oblivious as life is never meant to last

Time will be done one day

Time will mean nothing

or maybe something to those who find our stories

The last time you see a loved one

do not neglect your heart

Make the last time a powerful start

The Capture

You didn't know it,

but you won me when you found me

You didn't know it,

but you grew with me when you kept me

because you loved me for me

I bet you didn't know it,

and although you don't think it's true,

I am the one who captured you

PART IV: THE AWAKENING

Expressions of Silence

She sits and watches

learning and waiting

Silence is her only true expression

Peeking through the grasses

like the tigress and her prey

She ponders what it is like

to speak her life aloud for just once

Just once

She clings to a desperate hope

believing one day

her expressions of silence

can become expressions of her own voice

Terrified

An empty page with a blank world spill before me,

shadowing over me like bloody intentions

Disturbed by malice, highways roll out

through dangerous mountains of treachery

A flickering torch dies out on the wall as I wait

I am the hand that must stoke the flames

I am the shaking legs and weak knees of unending pain

Everything about that dying, flickering flame

looks too much like me

and I am terrified of more pain and sorrow

If I move too fast, I get caught

If I move too slow, I lose the race

Where is the hope for me?

Where is the future of my dreams?

It is up to me

So, I will pick up the torch anyway

and step out one foot before the other

until change becomes reality

And although the future may seem bleak

It is not empty

because the hope of it lives inside me

I'm terrified

but I will bring this flame back to life

A Neighboring Hope

I have dark skin

I have light skin

I have tattoos

I have stretch marks, too

I have scars from life

My skin is perfect

My skin is flawed

I have skin different from others

After all,

we're not all from the same mother's

I have a mind

I have dreams

I have things I do and keep

I too, want to work for what I want and need

I eat food like you

I eat different foods

I cook and dance, too

I read slow

I read fast

I read what I want

because stories are meant to last

I walk slow

I walk fast

I walk how I want to make the time pass

I breathe in nature

I stay indoors

I am who I am

and even get bored

And though some may not know me

I know them

because they have come against me

for being me

for being different than them

Deep inside

I have a neighboring hope

that another human

can appreciate me for me

my darkness,

my lightness,

my flaws,

my reading,

my cooking,

my dancing,

my walking,

my stretch marks

and even my scars,

when I am in nature or indoors,

even when I get bored

My History
Ashamed

It was taken from me

Who I am

Where I'm from

My people, my past, my history

Everything that helped shape me into who I am

Robbed, stomped on, silenced

Why do you not want to hear about my people?

Our pain

Our past

Our history

The heart is a fickle thing

Yes, but humanity is not

My humanity is not negotiable

Nor should it be silenced

We can teach to overcome hate by learning our history

Or we can silence the voices carrying the past atrocities

If teaching history hurts so much,

then silencing voices surely breeds fear

Fear can be overcome with knowledge,

and only love can overcome pain

Rekindled

I spoke up

I spoke out

You shut my mouth with your clout

I wrote it down,

pushed it out

You stomped it down,

blew the fires out

You want adoration

I want freedom from oppression

How long will it take

in your twisted obsessions?

You cut the hands off,

then the feet,

but you failed when giving

nourishment and meat

You blinded inquisitive hopes and dreams

and fought to conquer hearts and minds

You bled souls dry

so, they believe hunger is blessed

You fed a book of lies

and failed at the rest

So, go ahead,

cut off my hands and feet

Shut my mouth

Dash my hopes and dreams

You will never own my heart and mind

My soul will grow in defiance

of your wicked kind

And one day,

it won't just be me

One day,

the voices will

wail and shout

and take your clout

and steal your hopes and dreams,

because you believed

in your obsessions

over freedom from oppression

Just wait and see

The Persuasion

You will buy this lie

You will take this pain

You will do as I say

and never reclaim who you are

You will go here

You will do those things

You will learn this and that

You will follow the time given to you

You will live the rules set upon you

You will eat, breathe, and sleep as you are told

But what if I told you

you can also be persuaded

to buy hope with no money

and power with no clout

You can grow and thrive

in whom you are

and who you were created to be

There is a purpose ingrained within you

that no persuasion can take

and no force can kill

Nothing can hinder your hope

because the persuasion of its power

is not seen,

it is lived and breathed

Prism of Darkness

Hope and joy have lost their majestic glow

and peace has nowhere to go

The freedom of speech has become bars of prison

Integrity no longer has a vision

Eyes have lost their sight

because what looks real is full of lies

Ears cannot hear

because false truths are full of derision

The mouth utters words

but they fall into a chasm of darkness

and those who speak out

are thrust into prisons of silence

The mind is taught nothing

but endless chatter

to keep our focus from what matters

We are living

but have lost the will to live it

The prism of colors plunge

into the prism of darkness

Feed the Machine

I want to take a walk and breathe the air

I don't want to sit online and stare

Instead of stepping back to think

we are trained to drink

a double-edged sword

that clinks an clanks

it offers no clout or power

Tell me why our eyes cling to these lies?

And when you step offline,

it aches and moans

it groans and slows,

and you start all over again

The treachery never ends

A cog in the wheel can split and break

and the wheel will keep turning

until servants do not take

And when the cogs are all broken

and hopeless due to delusions,

the wheel spins and turns

to create more illusions

It may be round, but will never be whole

It may be loud, but it only drains the soul

You think you are missing out

but while the real world turns about

our lives are sucked dry

by an entity fed by greed

Our blood is drained dry

by the machine that needs to be fed

The Soul of Writing

The world wants the writers

endowed with powerful soul

screaming through their talent

They want to breathe hope or travesty

with pain or pleasure, tears or laughter

But greed wants what has always been written

to the same audience because

selling a new vision outside the box of the profits

shows there's no faith in the audience

as it screams for something different

And we are screaming

but the ocean is vast and wide

In the end,

due to entities greed

robots are writing books

because working outside the box

to keep soul in the writing

means more in profits than the humans

who are the creatives of the soul of writing

How Can I Serve You?

My body is complicated

A fearless progression of miracles,

stout with power, hope and strength

Why are you in charge of me?

A life is given to just be,

a life is blessed with courage and productivity

Yet you are in charge of me

What am I?

Do I have rights over me?

You've taken my right to think for myself,

you've boasted the rights to your hypocrisies

A tragedy you've become

fed by your policies, your ideologies,

your ambitions of control

You've no concept of how complicated we are

Yet you stand on your mountains of lies

telling us we should just be

what you want us to be,

that we have no right to our own bodies,

our own will,

our hopes and dreams.

Tell me,

how can I serve you again?

But this is how I WILL serve you...

I'll catapult knowledge to the dark corners

of your base that oppress lives

I'll stand on the highest mountain top,

screaming how the darkness knows you by name

I'll maintain my education,

my career progressions

I'll run my own businesses

and employ like-minded people

to help educate, inform, and liberate

And then,

when I am old,

I will look back at the lives I helped save

because I refused to serve you,

your religion,

your ideologies,

your hypocrisies

And those liberated will carry on

encouraging others and teach

that all bodies do not belong

to anyone else but their own

Now then,

would you like this served hot or cold?

Maps of Lies

Knowledge is slowly taken away

so, the world cannot seek what it wants

Why, over time,

do laws contradict what was taught?

So now I'm not allowed to gain the knowledge I want?

Darkness is shrouded by mystery,

cloaked with ignorant hysteria,

feeding off stupidity

I thought the light was more powerful than the darkness

That's what we have been taught

But the light is denied to those desperate to see

If only I had a flashlight to see through the darkness

If only I had a beacon, a flame, a flickering hope!

Would I be the dark one?

Or is the darkness really the light shining

on only those deemed to have value

except for me

We all have human eyes

yet see humanity in different lights

Darkness hates the stories

of knights with swords

who bring light back into the world

because humanity's hope comes from knowledge

and the cruel don't like swords

that demolish their darkness

Tired Empire

I tried to run but could only fall

My feet were not made for dictated ambitions

They were never made to be ruled at all

In their eyes, I burned water like bitter disappointment

I could do nothing right at all

I tried to climb the ladder of my hopeful dreams

I conformed, compartmentalized and schemed

I grew thin to their liking and styles

I lived sickly and deprived

I had times of blessed sustenance, too

I took the classes of etiquette with expectation

I grew weak and tired from the never-ending grind

but I just wanted to make a living

I lost more than I gained

and respect for myself

I gained more than I lost at times

endowed with self-doubt

I did it all to mean something for them

to stay on the clock

When I spoke up,

it was taken into consideration

but the ladder only held the voices who mattered

I tried to teach

Did they listen?

No, not at all

I've tried it all

So, when I fell,

I lied in the sand and stared at the clouds

weak and gave out

THE LAW OF BROKEN

When I fell,

the waves lapped my naked feet

and something raged within me

when I thought I had died

I fell again and again

to bring myself back to life

I fell, and reclaimed,

pieces of me that had been torn from my life

The weight of expectations

was always too great for me to carry

Who can carry it all?

Who wants the constant worry of the fall?

To hell with it all!

The weight of my sorrows

led to paths of undecisive confusion

So, I stand at the water's edge

and kiss the world

I stand at the water's edge

lingering with purpose, breathing again

I once was young,

but now am old,

and my empire is tired

I remember all my falls

Now I gaze up at the stars

as the sea laps my naked feet

After all, not all shoes were made for me

I was blind a long time

but now,

now I see

How Not to See

I looked through a hole in a wall

It was dark, unruly and dank, like a dreary Autumn

It promised things sight unseen

It lied to stay relevant with meaning

The harder I looked the more I wanted to see

The harder I pressed against the wall

the more my eyes screamed

Until one day, finally,

my soul cried out

One day, finally,

I pushed myself off the wall

and turned around to face a true Autumn

with glorious colors, hope and warmth,

with crisp breezes that led me away from the wall

The world opened to a vast horizon

the hills rolled and sank under the sun

the world breathed fervor like the rising dawn

and as my eyes focused on the splendor before me

I began to see more clearly

I saw a whole world

instead of looking through a hole in a wall

We think we are so smart

that we can hide and cover up

or show a snippet of little things

and make the world think it's big,

but it's not

If you want to see,

you have to get off the wall

you have to turn around and face the horizon

because if not,

I can tell you how not to see

by continuing to believe

a wall with a tiny hole of minimal perspective

is even big at all

Dust of my Bones

You came out of me screaming and shaking

In that moment,

the world was new again, to me

I breathed and lived with a hope for you,

for your future to begin anew,

and I wanted the best for you

But as time grew, life grew hard too,

and the weight of its unending grief barraged you,

with pain and sorrows, too,

and you wondered if it would ever end

With every choice and decision that was made

you had to choose too,

and learn that all roads are not straight,

and all roads do not lead the right way,

and some roads can lead us astray

to more sorrows and pain

As you grew, you had to hike through life

barefoot at times on jagged rocks,

and rocks of uncertainty,

and there are always rocks that hurt us all,

and many of us fall

We're only human, after all

Some rocks you kept, some rocks you tossed

And I fell to my knees in agony watching your pain,

while the shackles of life forced you

to face demons all on your own

The roads spilled pains we never knew existed

and ripped us apart for a while

And sometime, along the way,

THE LAW OF BROKEN

you grew armor of great strength

cloaked with your perseverance,

and even though you bled,

you experienced the soft hope of joy

and breathed in laughter and dreams

like there were no tomorrow,

and your eyes were lit with desires only you could feel

but I felt them too,

because I believed in you and still do

You learned lessons only you will ever know

and deep inside,

you are a deeply breathing, living soul

and one day,

you will share what you learned with the world,

because someone will come along

who needs your hope

As you continue to grow

I don't want you to worry

about the roads you may face

I don't want you to fear

the pain of jagged rocks

For we all must walk through life on them

and some of us have the right shoes

and some do not

I want you to continue moving forward

no matter what

I want you to continue pursuing your dreams

no matter who believes

Because there are always choices we will make

til the day we die,

and there are always roads to take

and we may never know why

Sometimes there are crossroads of disbelief,

and it's part of being human

but there is relief,

because as time passes

you will look back and see

how every little chore or road

brought you to this moment

so, you can breathe, live, and hope

It's okay if you feel like giving up

It's okay if life is too hard at times

and you just want to cry

It's okay to look back and say:

it was shit and I hate it all,

but this is what I learned from all those falls

Because one day, my dear child,

we will all be gone to dust

even as the world lingers on

So, you need to know that I am proud of you

no matter what

Burn it Off

I wore a hideous reprieve, and it was not me

It sunk inside me and lived, and breathed

It clawed in my mind sight unseen

It beckoned me to follow

but it only begat great sorrow

The gown hugged me and kissed my curves

The shroud was dark and uneven

in uncertain spurts

It sunk to my soul and no matter

how hard I screamed nothing came out

I cried in pain, could not move about

I turned to see everyone like me

who listened, groped it, and believed

I stared hard at this travesty,

these lies that fed me deep inside

It fed me with delusion,

but I starved, yet came back for more

It fed me with delirious dreams not of my soul

So, I turned around and saw

the shroud of my elegant gown

caught upon a pike of great impressions

And no matter how hard I tried to move forward,

the pike grew and grew

into more heated obsessions

Until finally,

I saw the best of me tainted and dead,

bleeding and screaming,

and I turned around, ripped the gown

and bloodied my fingers until flames burst out

I burned it off and it screamed out

THE LAW OF BROKEN

I slid out of the lying shroud,

the beautiful gown that whispered

I love you

but it did not love me for me

it never knew me or who I wanted to be

I would rather walk naked and alone

than continue living in a public world

where everything is about a lustful look

or a scheming, hopeless endeavor

In fact,

there are bottomless pits to vain endeavors

This gown is not who I am

and it is not growing back

I burned it off and will not look back

Spark the Flame

You cannot think of it all

You don't know what will happen

or how hard you will fight

for your future, your rights, and even your life

They say:

A small piece of dry kindling can spark a flame

And we are not delicate flowers

We are raging flames of unending power

We'll burn so others see our light

and the flames will be so hot

the blind will feel them no matter what

The Law of Broken

It's such a small thing,

but a trickle of water

eventually wears down stone

And then water

can break apart homes

and scatter bones

Water undermines foundations

built of stone,

creeping in, ruling this world

It conquers shadows

and screams never heard

It drowns out sorrows,

hiding caverns of pain

It's reckless and full of

malice and derision,

delightful in its acquisitions

It's soulless in its quest

to partake and break,

to lie and say it can heal,

but really, it just takes

It wants to keep growing

but hurt people know-

that even a little trickle

may soon become a catastrophic blow

And the law of broken

will continue to consume and grow

www.ingramcontent.com/pod-product-compliance
Lightning Source LLC
LaVergne TN
LVHW092232110526
838202LV00092B/13